# Talk Football

# Talk Football

## WRITTEN BY A WOMAN FOR WOMEN WHO WANT TO SPEAK AMERICA'S GRIDIRON LANGUAGE

*She's Got Game!*

*Alice Nicholas*

by Alice Nicholas
Pecan Row Press/Jackson

**TALK FOOTBALL**

www.talkfootball.biz

Copyright © 2006 by Alice G. Nicholas

**Pecan Row Press**
603 Duling Avenue, Suite 205
Jackson, MS 39216
Email: info@pecanrowpress.com
www.pecanrowpress.com

Printed in China

Library of Congress Cataloging - in - Publication Data

Nicholas, Alice
    Talk Football: written by a woman for women who want to
    speak America's gridiron language / by Alice Nicholas.

ISBN - 13: 978-0-9795187-0-6

ISBN - 10: 0-9795187-0-9

1. Football  2. Sports - United States  3. Women - United States
    I. Title

Artist:  Janie Davis
Editor:  Joe Maxwell
Graphic Designer:  Jessica Wood
Illustrator:  Mark Nicholas

TO

MY HUSBAND, MARK,
AND OUR THREE SONS,
TAYLOR, REED AND JAMEY,
WHO ALL PLAYED FOOTBALL...

I GET IT!

# Acknowledgements

Thanks to the following coaches who profoundly influenced my family's lives: Buddy Bartling, Trey Bayliss, Ricky Black, Nick Brewer, Rusty Burke, Jack Carlisle, Buddy Crosby, Will Crosby, Joe Dallas, Joey Hydrick, Brian Jones, Chan McCloud, Gary Noble, Fred Perrett, Paul Purvis, and Trey Watkins.

Thanks to those who critiqued this book: Ricky and Linda Black, Lucius Cook, Sylvester Croom, Tim and Vicki Ellis, Peter Glover, Will Glover, Ken Toler, Les and Mary Triplett, Billy Watkins and Robert Wilson.

Special thanks to: Angelyn Cannada and Reed Hogan, for their photographs; Janie Davis, for her beautiful watercolors; Mark Nicholas, for his illustrations; Jessica Wood, for her creative design; and Joe Maxwell for his guidance and editing.

I am humbly grateful for my friend's and family's support, encouragement and prayers: Carole Bailey, Sandra Barnes, Barb Currie, Nick Davis, Sherye Green, Billy and Francine Greenlee, Ellen and Brad McCay, Deborah Newman, Lisa Paris, Donna and Adam Parks, Lisa Sledge; and my sons, Taylor, Reed and Jamey, along with Taylor's wife, Katie.

ATTITUDES ARE CONTAGIOUS!

# Talk Football

WRITTEN BY A WOMAN
FOR WOMEN WHO WANT TO
SPEAK AMERICA'S GRIDIRON LANGUAGE

## By Alice Nicholas

Watercolors by Janie Davis
Illustrations by Mark Nicholas

"You're not raising boys, you're raising men."

Mrs. Jane Baird
Mother of Five Sons

# Talk Football

## TABLE OF CONTENTS

| | | |
|---|---|---|
| Introduction | | xii |
| Chapter 1 | American Football's History | 1 |
| Chapter 2 | The Football Field | 6 |
| Chapter 3 | Football Gear | 10 |
| Chapter 4 | The Players | 16 |
| Chapter 5 | The Coaches | 26 |
| Chapter 6 | The Score | 30 |
| Chapter 7 | Game Time | 34 |
| Chapter 8 | Officials, Play Rulings and Penalties | 40 |
| Chapter 9 | How A Typical Game May Go | 54 |
| Chapter 10 | The X's and O's | 64 |
| Official's Signals | | 80 |
| Gridiron Glossary | | 82 |
| Football Field Diagram | | 112 |
| Endnotes | | 113 |

# Introduction

My earliest football memories are of sitting next to my father watching games on our black-and-white television set. He kept me entertained, cheering for his favorite teams and reminiscing about his own football days. On occasion, my father took my mother, sister, and myself to college games. We enjoyed dressing up and visiting with our friends, but we ladies watched the clock for the game to hurry up and end.

In high school I became friends with a good-looking football player. I wanted to be cool and "talk football" so I went to the library to read up on the sport. I checked out a book, but couldn't make myself finish it. Years later I married that football player and was blessed with three more football players. When my oldest began playing the sport in the fifth grade, I realized the family conversations were quickly moving over my head. So, once again, I trudged through more books, but I would have rather been reading my middle son's boating magazines.

By the time my youngest reached junior high I realized the positive effect this vigorous sport and its coaches were making on my sons and their teammates. THEY WERE BUILDING CHARACTER; LEARNING TEAMWORK; GAINING LEADERSHIP SKILLS, DISCIPLINE AND SACRIFICE; UNDERSTANDING HOW TO WIN AND, WHEN THEY LOST, HOW TO LEARN FROM THEIR MISTAKES AND NEVER QUIT.

While they were building character, I was on my knees praying for their protection, washing dirty uniforms, cooking hearty meals, reading everything I could about the sport and attending every game. My friends sitting next to me in the stands would ask me questions, assuming I knew the answers since this was my third son playing ball. I realized we all had a lot to learn and I decided to write a simple book that a novice could understand. It was a greater undertaking than I imagined, and with the help of my husband, sons, coaches and friends, I am able to share the foundation of this complicated game, so you too can "TALK FOOTBALL."

# AMERICAN

*Football's History*

## CHAPTER ONE

# American Football's History

Football's origins have been variously attributed to the ancient Chinese, Greeks, Romans and Japanese as early as 200 B.C., and its rise and fall in popularity has been as turbulent as a king's reign. In the 1100s, England's King Henry II, preferring archery to football, forbade any men to play the kicking game, and banned it for 400 years. Nonetheless, by the 1800s a sport resembling modern day soccer had evolved and in 1823 an intramural game was played in Rugby, England where a player illegally caught a punt and ran to score. The rule infraction was the genesis of rugby, named for the town in which the game was founded.

Not yet football, the popularity of soccer and rugby spread throughout the world. By the mid-1800s, eastern colleges in the United States had combined the two sports and exchanged a round ball for an oval shape. Representatives from many East-Coast colleges, including Harvard and Yale universities, met together in 1876 at the Massasoit Convention to establish guidelines for the new American sport they named football and formed the Intercollegiate Football Association (IFA). Although rules had been made, there were serious injuries and deaths due to, in part, the offense's mass formations in the "flying wedge" and the defense's gang tackling. The violence of the sport led game critics in a movement to abolish football. Schools rapidly withdrew their membership and the IFA folded in 1894.

In 1905 and 1906, President Teddy Roosevelt held two conferences at the White House with representatives from schools

including New York University, Yale, Harvard, Princeton and
Pennsylvania to discuss reform. Rule committees made changes
to protect the players, thereby protecting the new American
sport and the Intercollegiate Athletic Association was estab-
lished. The name was changed to the National Collegiate
Athletic Association (NCAA) in 1910.

While the sport gained momentum among local athletic clubs
across America, problems arose because there were no regula-
tions for these professional teams. Players could leave one team
and immediately join another; some played for their college and
an athletic club at the same time; and unethical owners enticed
players with money. In 1920, eleven athletic clubs met in
Canton, Ohio at the Jordan and Hupmobile showroom, forming
a governing board to regulate the teams called the American
Professional Football Association. Two years later they renamed
it the National Football League (NFL).

For the next forty years other football leagues tried to compete
against the NFL, but none were successful until millionaire
Lamar Hunt backed the American Football League (AFL) in
1960. Conflicts arose between leagues because now there were
two leagues wanting the same TV contracts and college draft

3

choices. Six years later, representatives from the AFL and NFL agreed to combine the two leagues and split into two conferences. The winners of the two conferences would play against each other for the championship. The first world championship game was played in 1967 in Los Angeles, California. One year later America knew this championship game as the Super Bowl.

Football has evolved into a billion-dollar industry, serving both metropolitan and small-town lifestyles, boasting millions of spectators cheering on their favorite teams. The ancient Chinese, Greeks, Romans and Japanese would be astonished at this captivating game and its athletes who are the gladiators of today.

---

**FRITZ POLLARD**

AFRICAN-AMERICAN FOOTBALL PIONEER

Born in 1894, Frederick Douglass Pollard grew up in Chicago, playing football at Northwestern, Harvard, Dartmouth and Brown. He was the first African-American to play in the Rose Bowl and to be named All-American halfback. With the Akron Pros, he was the first African-American player/co-coach in what later became the NFL. When African-Americans were quietly prohibited from playing professional football from 1934-1946, Pollard organized a successful black pro football team called the Brown Bombers. "I still say that Fritz Pollard did more to advance the idea of the best-against-the-best-regardless-of-color than any single man in the business," stated Herschel Day, the Bomber's former manager.[i] Frederick Douglass Pollard was inducted posthumously into the Pro Football Hall of Fame, Class of 2005.

---

## WALTER CAMP
### THE FATHER OF AMERICAN FOOTBALL

In 1876, Walter Camp played on Yale's rugby team against Harvard and was instrumental in creating today's game of football. He was on every rule committee from 1876 until 1911, initiating eleven men on the field of play, the line of scrimmage, the system of downs, and the point system. When football was under attack for its physical roughness, Camp introduced the forward pass.[ii]

# THE *Football Field*

## CHAPTER TWO

# The Football Field

The FOOTBALL FIELD, also called the GRIDIRON, historically has had many lines resembling a pattern or grid; today the term "gridiron" can refer to the game of football itself.

The grass or a man-made grass-like material covering the FIELD OF PLAY measures 100 x 53 1/3 yards. Five-yard markers run across the field's width, measuring up to the 50-yard line, called MIDFIELD; the markers then reverse back to the 45-yard line, the 40-yard line, down to the 5-yard line.

Each football play starts in the area between the HASH MARKS, the broken lines that run down the center of both sides of the field in 1-yard sequences. SIDELINES, two stripes that run the length of the field, form the outer boundary lines of the playing field.

The line at each end of the playing field that a player must cross with the ball to score is called the GOAL LINE. Ten yards behind each goal line is the END LINE that marks the end of the playing field. The distance between the goal line and the end line, called the END ZONE, is the area where a player must enter to score. Positioned at each goal line are GOAL POSTS, U-shaped structures. Teams kick extra points or field goals over the bar and through its uprights.

PYLONS, four orange markers, are positioned at each corner of the end zones to mark the goal line and end line.

The sign at the end of the football field is the SCOREBOARD. It displays each team's score, the game clock, who has the ball, the current down, the distance to a new first down, and each team's remaining time outs (TOL — time out left).

*(Note: football field diagram, page 112.)*

The RED ZONE is an unmarked area between the end zone and the 20-yard line. When teams are in the red zone, it is a crucial time for both, because they are either within 20 yards of scoring, or 20 yards of being scored upon.

# Football Gear

## CHAPTER THREE

# Football Gear

The two types of football gear are the uniforms that players wear and the equipment they use.

**UNIFORMS** protect players from injuries and differentiate teams. The HELMET is hard plastic with shock absorbing materials inside.

A CHINSTRAP, FACEMASK and MOUTHPIECE are attached; different player positions require different facemasks. SHOULDER PADS cushion the shoulders and upper rib cage; linemen usually wear larger shoulder pads, backs and receivers wear smaller, less cumbersome pads.

PANTS have pads to protect the hips, knees and thighs. CLEATED SHOES promote traction on the football field; the field's surface and condition determine the type of cleats used. The JERSEY displays the team's colors and a player's number, which are generally determined by the player's position. The home team usually wears white and the visiting team usually wears a darker color jersey.

Optional uniform parts include a FLAK JACKET to guard the ribs and sternum. A COWBOY or ROLL COLLAR can be fit atop the shoulder pads to prevent neck backlash. ARM PADS cushion the forearms, and GLOVES protect hands and help backs and receivers grip the ball.

**EQUIPMENT** used by players and referees to play the game are the football, the kicking tee and the down marker and yardage chains.

A FOOTBALL is a prolate spheroid that is made of four panels of grained leather sewn with a row of white laces. A KICKING TEE is a small stand used to hold the ball upright on kick-offs.

DOWN MARKERS and CHAINS are used by the referee's chain crew to let teams and fans know whatever down the team is playing. The down marker is a sign on top of a stick that displays 1st, 2nd, 3rd, or 4th down, and the sign moves every play with the ball; a 10-yard chain connects two sticks and measures the yardage required for a first down; the chains don't move until a first down is made or possession of the ball changes.

# WHAT'S IN A NUMBER?

JERSEY NUMBERS are usually determined by PLAYERS' POSITIONS.

An offensive player wearing a number between 50-79, who catches a pass, is considered an "INELIGIBLE RECEIVER" and is penalized 5 yards and the loss of one down.

| OFFENSE | JERSEY NUMBERS | DEFENSE |
|---|---|---|
| Quarterback, Punter, Kicker | 1-19 | |
| Wide Receivers | 11-19 | |
| Running Backs | 20-49 | Defensive Backs |
| Center | 50-59 | Linebackers |
| Offensive Guards & Tackles | 60-79 | Defensive Linemen |
| Wide Receivers & Tight Ends | 80-89 | |
| | 90-99 | Linebackers & Defensive Linemen |

# The Players

## CHAPTER FOUR

# The Players

Players are trained to perform with knowledge, power, speed and emotion. Those who display an enthusiastic desire for the game create contagious, winning attitudes for their team and encourage spectator participation. One player cannot win a ball game; it takes an entire team.

Teams may have an unlimited number of players, but only 11 take the field for OFFENSE, DEFENSE and SPECIAL TEAMS. At the beginning of every play, 11 players from each team line up in formation against one another at the line of scrimmage (LOS).

---

### OFFENSIVE PLAYER KEY

⊘ OFFENSIVE LINEMEN
  C — Center
  LG — Left Guard
  LT — Left Tackle
  RG — Right Guard
  RT — Right Tackle

⊘ ENDS
  TE — Tight End
  WR — Wide Receiver

⊘ BACKS
  QB — Quarterback
  RB — Running Back
    FB — Fullback
    TB or HB — Tailback or Halfback

---

## TEAM CAPTAINS

Each team selects captains, an honor that recognizes players' skill and leadership qualities. The captains meet at the center of the field before the game for the coin toss. The visiting team calls the toss and the winner of the toss chooses either to:

1. Receive the kickoff and go on offense first;
2. Kickoff and go on defense first; or
3. Defer, allowing the coin-toss winner to choose in the second half.

During the game the captains are the only players who can talk to the officials (except for requesting time outs), and can ask for an explanation of the penalty and what player committed the foul. The captain of the non-offending team has the option to accept or decline the penalty.

---

### DEFENSIVE PLAYER KEY

✗ DEFENSIVE LINEMEN
      NG or NT — Nose Guard or Nose Tackle
      DT — Defensive Tackle
      DE — Defensive End

✗ LINEBACKERS
      MLB — Middle Linebacker
      LB — Linebacker

✗ DEFENSIVE BACKS
      CB — Cornerback
      S — Safety
         FS — Free Safety
         SS — Strong Safety

---

## OFFENSE

O ffense possesses the ball and stands across the line of scrimmage from the defense their objective is to run or pass the ball down the field and across the defense's end zone to score a touchdown.

- OFFENSIVE LINEMEN (O Line) are large, strong and agile; seven players must be positioned on the line of scrimmage to block the defense's effort, and five are linemen.

  - $C$ Center - stands in the middle of the line and snaps the ball between his legs to the quarterback to start each play.

  - $G$ Guards - left and right guards play on either side of the center. They block defensive linemen and open holes for running backs.

  - $T$ Tackles - left and right tackles play outside the guards and block defensive linemen, linebackers or defensive ends.

- ENDS play outside the offensive tackles, blocking or receiving passes.

  - $TE$ Tight End - positioned beside one tackle "tight to the end of the line"; therefore this side of the line is called the strong side.

  - $WR$ Wide Receiver (Wide Out or Split End) - a quick and agile player with good hands to catch the ball.

# A BASIC OFFENSIVE FORMATION

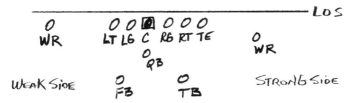

 BACKS set up behind the linemen to run or catch the ball, and sometime block.

**Q B** Quarterback - offensive leader who calls the plays, runs with the ball, hands the ball off or passes the ball to another back.

**R B** Running backs - positioned behind the quarterback to run or catch the ball and block.

**F B** Fullback - main blocker for the quarterback on passing and running plays and for the tailback on the running plays.

**T B** Tailback (Halfback) - primarily runs with the ball and catches short passes, but also blocks for the quarterback and fullback.

**W B** Wingback (Flanker) - extra back that may line up off the tight end's shoulder in a wing formation in the backfield.

## DEFENSE

The defense stands across the line of scrimmage from the offense; their objective is to try to stop the offense from scoring and to gain possession of the ball.

X DEFENSIVE LINEMEN (D Line) are strong and aggressive players; they position themselves on the line of scrimmage to avoid the offense's blocks and tackle the ball carrier.

NG Nose Guard (Nose Tackle) - plays across from the offensive center.

DT Defensive Tackles - play on either side of the nose guard and across from the offensive guards or tackles.

DE Defensive Ends - play on the side of the defensive tackles and across from the offensive tackles or tight end.

X LINEBACKERS are versatile players that stand behind the defensive linemen; they try to "read" where the ball is going in order to tackle runners who get past the defensive linemen.

MLB Middle Linebacker - stands in the middle facing the quarterback and calls the defensive plays.

OLB Outside Linebacker - plays to the outside behind the defensive end.

# A BASIC DEFENSIVE FORMATION

X DEFENSIVE BACKS, known as "the secondary", are quick and able to make open-field tackles or cover wide receivers (i.e. prevent them from catching a pass).

CB Cornerbacks - play the corner sides of the field.

S Safety - play the deepest part of the backfield and are the last line of defense before their end zone.

FS Free Safety - positioned toward the center of the backfield.

SS Strong Safety - positioned across from the offensive tight end.

## SPECIAL TEAMS

The special teams are 11 players specializing in executing or stopping kicking plays. The place kicker, punter, holder and returner are the primary special team players.

PLACE KICKER - attempts all his team's field goals and extra points, therefore he needs to kick strong, steady and accurate.

PUNTER - must be able to catch the center's long snaps, punt the ball long, high and accurate, placing it near the opponent's goal line.

HOLDER - catches the ball snapped from the center; stands the ball on end for the place kicker to attempt field goals and extra points.

RETURNER - must have good hands to catch the ball, and be quick and agile in order to avoid his opponents on kick-off and punt teams.

ONSIDE KICKS are often used at the end of close ball-games. These are short kicks that must travel at least 10 yards. The kicking team tries to regain possession of the ball by either catching it or covering the returner.

A SQUIB KICK refers to a ball kicked to flutter and roll erratically.

KICKOFF TEAM / KICK RETURN TEAM take the field to begin the game, the second half, and after every score. The Kickoff team's place kicker boots the ball off a tee downfield; all 11 players then try to tackle the kick returner, who tries to catch the ball and run it toward the end zone while his team blocks for him.

PUNT TEAM / PUNT RETURN TEAM take the field when a team fails to make a 1st down after four attempts. The punt team's punter drops the ball onto his foot, kicking it downfield; the punter and his teammates then try to tackle the punt returner, who attempts to run the ball toward the end zone while his team blocks for him.

FIELD GOAL TEAMS take the field if the offensive coach believes they are in a situation where it is unlikely they'll score a touchdown and need to try for a 3-point field goal. On offense, the long snapper snaps the ball about 7 yards back from the line of scrimmage to the holder, who then stands the ball on end for the place kicker to attempt to kick the ball through the goal posts, while his team blocks the defense. On defense, 11 players that try to block the place kicker's attempt.

EXTRA POINT TEAMS take the field after a touchdown has been earned and attempts to kick the ball through the goal posts to earn 1 point. On offense, the ball is snapped back to the holder who quickly stands the ball on end for the kicker to kick the ball through the goal posts. On defense, 11 players that try to block the kicker's attempts.

# The Coaches

## CHAPTER FIVE

# The Coaches

Coaches prepare their players to win games by wearing a variety of hats as teacher, preacher, strategist, psychologist, disciplinarian, mentor and motivator. They study videos to learn about their own team's habits and those of their opponents and draw plays to map out how to beat the opposing team. Coaches prepare their players' minds and bodies for competitive game days.

The HEAD COACH leads the team and is held responsible for the outcome of the game.

COACHING COORDINATORS are the primary assistants in charge of specific squads, such as the offense, defense and special teams. A coordinator may be on the sidelines or in the press box during the game.

COACHING ASSISTANTS are in charge of certain divisions in the squads, such as the offensive or defensive linemen, offensive or defensive backs, etc.

---

"Iron sharpens iron, so one man sharpens another." [iii]
—Proverbs 27:17

---

"All NFL players, past and present, owe a great debt to the coaches and other volunteers who made football a positive, life-affirming experience when we were young." [iv]

*Gene Upshaw*
Hall of Fame NFL Player
NFL Players Association
Executive Director

"Mama wanted me to be a preacher. I told her coachin' and preachin' were a lot alike." [v]

*Coach Paul "Bear" Bryant*
Former Head Coach
The University of Alabama

"It's easy to have faith in yourself and have discipline when you're a winner, when you're number one. What you've got to have is faith and discipline when you're not yet a winner." [vi]

*Coach Vince Lombardi*
Former Head Coach
Green Bay Packers

# The Score

## CHAPTER SIX

# The Score

There are five ways to earn points or **SCORE** in football.

A TOUCHDOWN, worth 6 POINTS, is the most a team can earn in one play. The offense's objective is to score a touchdown by running the ball, catching a pass, or falling on a live ball in the end zone. A defensive player can also score a touchdown by gaining possession of the ball and crossing over the opponent's goal line.

After a team scores a touchdown, they have a chance to score again by either going for the extra point or a 2-point conversion.

The EXTRA POINT, worth 1 POINT, is also called a P.A.T., or point after touchdown. When "going for one," the ball is placed on the defense's 3-yard line for high school and college, and the 2-yard line for professional football. The place kicker must successfully kick the ball between the goal posts to be awarded 1 extra point.

The 2-POINT CONVERSION, worth 2 POINTS, is more of a challenge. When "going for two," the ball is placed on the defender's 3-yard line for high school and college and the 2-yard line for professional football. In one play, the offensive player must carry the ball over the goal line, or the quarterback must throw the ball to a teammate in the end zone. If successful, the offense is awarded 2 extra points.

A FIELD GOAL, worth 3 POINTS, is usually tried on an offensive team's fourth down, when they are close enough to the goal line that they believe they can placekick the ball through the goal posts. The holder kneels and holds the ball for the kicker to attempt to boot the ball between the goal posts. If successful, the offense is awarded 3 points.

A SAFETY, worth 2 POINTS, is awarded to the DEFENSE when they tackle the offensive ball carrier in his own end zone, or force the offense to commit a foul in his own end zone, or fumble the ball out of bounds in his own end zone.

"For when the One Great Scorer comes to mark against your name, he writes — not that you won or lost — but how you played the game."[vii]

Grantland Rice
Famous Sports Writer

"The difference between success & failure often depends on the last 5% of effort rather than the 95% that preceeds it."[viii]

Anonymous

# Game Time

## CHAPTER SEVEN

# Game Time

Game Time is divided into a FIRST HALF and a SECOND HALF, with a HALFTIME in between. There are FOUR QUARTERS in each game. The first and second quarters are in the first half; the third and fourth quarters are in the second half. Teams change the end zone they defend at the beginning of each quarter. High school and younger teams play 12-minute quarters and 48-minute games. College and professional teams play 15-minute quarters and 60-minute games.

The scoreboard's **GAME CLOCK** counts down each quarter by seconds. The clock counts down from 12 minutes to 0 for high school games and from 15 minutes to 0 for college and professional games. The quarter is over when the clock expires.

### START THE CLOCK

The clock starts when the ball is snapped. It runs when the ball carrier is tackled within the playing field not resulting in a change of ball possession. During kickoffs, the clock starts the moment the ball is touched by the kicker.

STOP THE CLOCK

The clock is stopped for the following reasons:
• A score
• A quarter ends
• A team time out has been requested
• A ball carrier is out of bounds
• A foul is committed
• A ruling is discussed
• A television commercial
• An incomplete pass
• An injured player
• An instant reply challenge
• The down markers moved for a new first down
• The ball changes possession between teams

TEAM TIME OUTS

Each team is permitted three time outs in each half of the game. When a time out is called, the game clock is stopped and both teams are allowed to go to the sidelines to rest and listen to their coach's instructions.
• A team may not call consecutive time outs without a play in-between.
• Time outs not used in the first half of the game cannot carry over into the second half.

## OVERTIME

When the score is tied, an extension of playing time is allowed to determine the winner. Rules for high school, college and professional games vary.

In HIGH SCHOOL, each team's offense starts at their opponent's 10-yard line with four plays to score. The team that scores the most wins.

In COLLEGE, each team's offense starts at their opponent's 25-yard line, and can have a maximum of two first downs. This process is repeated until the team that scores the most wins.

In PRO ball, a coin is tossed and the winning team chooses to go on offense or defense. A fifteen-minute quarter is set and "Sudden Death Overtime" starts with a kick off. Each team is allowed two time outs; and the first team to score wins. If neither team scores at the end of fifteen minutes, it remains a tie. The playoff games and Super Bowl games are an exception to this rule. They keep playing until one team scores to break the tie in order to advance to the playoffs or win the championship.

## PLAY CLOCK

A play clock runs independently of the game clock and is placed at each end zone to monitor the time each team takes between plays. The offense has 25 seconds between every down to start a play. If the clock winds down to zero before the ball is snapped, the offense is penalized 5 yards for a delay of game.

## CLOCK STRATEGIES
TOWARD THE END OF A GAME:

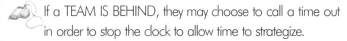 If a TEAM IS BEHIND, they may choose to call a time out in order to stop the clock to allow time to strategize.

If the OFFENSIVE TEAM IS BEHIND, they may choose to stop the clock by throwing quick passing plays and running out of bounds, or purposely throwing an incomplete pass.

If the TEAM IS AHEAD they may eat the clock up, or use up as much time on the clock as they can. For example, if a team is ahead by a slight margin in the 4th quarter, coaches may intentionally delay the game and take a 5-yard penalty so their opponents will have less time to score should they get the ball.

# OFFICIALS, PLAY RULINGS & *Penalties*

## CHAPTER EIGHT

# Officials, Play Rulings & Penalties

Officials are the keepers of the rules to insure player safety, fair play and good sportsmanship. There are four to seven officials who wear black-and-white striped shirts with white pants. The chief official, called the referee, wears a white hat and the other officials wear black hats. Each wears a whistle around his neck for starting and stopping each play.

The REFEREE officiates the coin toss and signals to the clock operator when to start the clock. He places the ball at the correct spot for the start of each play and stands in the offensive backfield behind the quarterback on the side of his throwing arm. He issues final rulings on all disputes, and makes the hand signals to tell the teams and spectators what foul and penalty has been called.

The UMPIRE rules on players' equipment before the game begins. He stands at the line of scrimmage to observe the offensive plays and maintains the score.

The HEAD LINESMAN marks the spot where the ball comes to rest and directs the chain crew. He stands at the line of scrimmage near a sideline to track the forward movement of the offensive team.

The LINE JUDGE carries a clock to keep the official game time in case the scoreboard clock fails. He stands at the line of scrimmage to observe all players on the line and their actions.

The SIDE JUDGE stands behind the defense to observe passing plays and determines where a ball went out of bounds when crossing the sidelines.

The BACK JUDGE determines where a ball went out of bounds when crossing the sidelines. During field goal and extra point attempts, he stands under one upright of the goal post to determine if the kick is good.

The FIELD JUDGE monitors the clock during time outs and intermission. He stands farthest back in the defensive backfield observing punts, kickoffs and deep passes.

# PLAY RULINGS
## SCORING

 TOUCHDOWN (6 POINTS) — player crossed over opponent's goal line with possession of the ball.

EXTRA POINT (1 POINT) — kicker kicked the ball between the goal posts after a touchdown.

2 POINT CONVERSION (2 POINTS) — player crossed the defender's goal line with possession of the ball after a touchdown.

FIELD GOAL (3 POINTS) — place kicker kicked the ball through the goal posts.

 SAFETY (2 POINTS) — awarded to the defense after they've tackled the offensive ball carrier in his own end zone, or after the offense commits a foul or fumbles the ball in their own end zone.

## TIME KEEPING

 START THE CLOCK — the clock starts when the ball is snapped or the moment the ball is touched by the kicker during kick-offs.

 TIME OUT — the game clock stops at this signal.

## GAME MANAGEMENT

 FIRST DOWN — the offense has gained the minimum 10 yards required in four plays.

 LOSS OF DOWN — the offense is penalized the loss of one down due to a foul.

 TOUCHBACK — a player gets possession of the ball in his own end zone and decides not to run the ball onto the field; kneeling on one knee, he downs the ball in his end zone and is awarded possession of the ball on the 20-yard line with a first down.

 NO GOOD — signifies an incomplete pass from the quarterback to his receiver; a declined penalty from the non-offending team; or a failed field goal attempt.

THE CHAIN CREW consists of three assistants to the officials who measure the offensive team's progress by using the chains and down markers to count the number of downs and to track the yardage required for a first down.

DOWNS — Each offensive play is called a DOWN. There are 1st, 2nd, 3rd or 4th downs.

The offense is allowed a series of 4 plays, or "downs," to move the ball 10 yards by either passing or running the ball. If they are successful in gaining 10 yards within 4 consecutive plays, the offense earns a "first down" and 4 more attempts to earn another first down by moving the ball toward their opponent's end zone.

If they fail to gain 10 yards within four plays, they lose possession of the ball to the opposing team.

**PENALTIES** are called for rule violations; a penalty moves the team that committed the foul further away from their opponent's goal line. When an official observes a foul, he signals by pulling a yellow flag out of his back pocket and tossing it into the air; the play continues until the official blows the whistle. The official and the referee discuss their observations and make a ruling.

When a team commits a FOUL during a single play, the captain of the non-offending team is given the opportunity to either accept or decline the penalty. If they accept the penalty, the offending team is moved backwards and the down is replayed. If they refuse the penalty, the down is used up and the play stands.

DOUBLE FOULS or OFF-SETTING PENALTIES, fouls on each team, cancel each other out and the down is repeated. An exception would be if one team commits a 5-yard penalty and the other commits a 15-yard penalty. The 5-yard penalty is ignored and the 15-yard penalty stands.

If the team commits MULTIPLE FOULS during a single play, only one of the penalties is accepted. The captain on the opposing team determines which penalty will be enforced.

## PENALTIES AT THE START OF THE PLAY

 DELAY OF GAME — the offense fails to begin the play within the time allowed, resulting in a 5-yard penalty and the down must be repeated.

 FALSE START — an offensive player illegally moves before the ball is snapped, resulting in a 5-yard penalty and the down must be repeated.

 OFFSIDES — an offensive player crosses the line of scrimmage before the ball is snapped; or

ENCROACHMENT — a defensive player crosses into the neutral zone and fails to get back in position before the ball is snapped, resulting in a loss of 5 yards and the down must be repeated.

 ILLEGAL MOTION — a player in the offensive backfield moves toward the line of scrimmage before the ball is snapped, resulting in a 5-yard penalty and the down must be repeated.

## BASIC PENALTIES DURING A PLAY

 HOLDING — an offensive player illegally grabs an opposing player resulting in a 10-yard penalty; or a defensive player illegally grabs an opposing player resulting in a 5-yard penalty. The down must be repeated for both offensive and defensive penalties.

 ILLEGAL USE OF HANDS — an offensive player illegally pushes or pulls the ball carrier forward, or hits his opponent in the head or neck to prevent a tackle, resulting in a 10-yard penalty and the down is repeated; if a defensive player illegally grabs or pulls an offensive player, it results in a 5-yard penalty and an automatic first down for the offense.

 INELIGIBLE RECEIVER DOWNFIELD — an offensive player wearing jersey numbers 50-79 moves downfield past the line of scrimmage to catch a pass resulting in a 5-yard penalty and the down must be repeated.

INTENTIONAL GROUNDING — the quarterback throws the ball, purposely missing his receiver in order to avoid being sacked, resulting in a 5-yard penalty and the loss of a down.

 PASS INTERFERENCE — a receiver tries to stop a defender from intercepting the ball rather than trying to catch the ball, resulting in a 10-yard penalty and the down must be repeated; if a receiver is hit, tackled, or grabbed before the ball reaches him, a first down is awarded to the offense at the site of the foul. If the interference occurs in the defense's end zone, the offense gets first down on the defense's 1-yard line.

 TRIPPING — a player uses any part of his body intentionally or unintentionally to trip an opposing player, resulting in 10-yard penalty and the loss of a down.

**BASIC PERSONAL FOULS** are received due to a player

demonstrating extreme force that might injure
another player, resulting in a 15-yard penalty. The
referee signals a "personal foul" and then calls the
specific foul and additional penalty.

FACEMASK — a player intentionally grabs an
opponent's facemask, resulting in a 15-yard penalty and an automatic first down. If a player unintentionally grabs an opponent's face mask, a 5-
yard penalty is called and the down is repeated.

CLIPPING — a player blocks an opponent from
behind, resulting in a 15-yard penalty and an automatic first down.

CHOP BLOCK — a defensive player is blocked,
and a second player blocks him below the waist,
resulting in a 15-yard penalty and the down is
repeated.

ILLEGAL BLOCK — a player blocks an opponent below the waist during an interception, fumble recovery, or kicking play, resulting in a 15-yard penalty and an automatic first down.

 ROUGHING THE KICKER — a defensive player hits the kicker as he is kicking the ball, resulting in a 15-yard penalty and an automatic first down.

 UNSPORTSMANLIKE CONDUCT — a player creates ill will by demeaning or threatening acts or language toward opponents, officials or spectators, resulting in a 15-yard penalty and an automatic first down.

# HOW A *Typical Game* MAY GO

## CHAPTER NINE

# How A Typical Game May Go

Thirty minutes prior to the game the UMPIRE visits each team in their locker rooms. At this time each team's head coach is responsible for verifying that all players are properly equipped and in compliance and if they have any unusual plays or formations they intend to use. Coaches may also bring up potential rule violations of their opponents picked up during scouting or film sessions. Meanwhile, both teams are on the field warming up, called PRE-GAME. Upon completion, they return to their locker rooms to listen to final game instructions from their coach.

At the beginning of the game, the COIN TOSS is held at midfield, and both teams' CAPTAINS are introduced. The REFEREE designates a captain from the VISITING team to call the coin when tossed. The team that wins the toss may choose to receive the kick off, kick off, or defer to the second half.

To START THE GAME, each team's SPECIAL TEAM squad of eleven players enters the field for the OPENING KICKOFF. The football is placed on a kicking tee to be kicked by the PLACE KICKER towards the receiving team's end of the field. Usually five players line up on each side of the place kicker. The kicking team can gain momentum by running two or three steps before the place kicker kicks the ball, but must stay behind the designated yard line until the ball is kicked. As they run downfield the KICKOFF RETURN team sets up their blocking formation for the KICK RETURNER. The ball must advance 10 yards before it is considered a live ball and fair game for either team. The receiving team's kick returner has a team of 10 players blocking to allow him to quickly return the ball down field, gaining as much yardage as possible. The special teams exit the field.

If the ball is kicked past the end zone or the kick returner catches the ball in his own end zone and touches his knee to the ground, the ball is dead. A TOUCHBACK is called and the ball is to be placed on the 20-yard line to start the next play. If the ball is kicked out of bounds before it reaches the goal line, and hasn't been touched, a penalty is called and it must be kicked again. When the kick returner is tackled, the ball is placed at the spot where the return ended.

The offensive and defensive teams run onto the field and both squads gather into a HUDDLE behind their line of scrimmage. The quarterback calls the offensive play, naming the SNAP COUNT. The defense's middle linebacker calls their plays to try and stop the offense from advancing the ball toward their end zone.

The offense and defense face opposite one another across the line of scrimmage. The quarterback tries to "read" the defense. If he believes it's necessary for his team to change the play, he may call an AUDIBLE prior to the snap. The quarterback shouts the snap count to indicate when he wants his center to snap the ball. The play begins at the snap. After the snap, the quarterback will hand off, pass or run the ball toward his opponent's end zone, and try to gain as much yardage as possible.

---

THE SNAP COUNT

The quarterback calls out a cadence or secret code to his teammates at the start of each play, which allows them to know when the center will snap the ball and what play they are to put into action.

Example:  Blue 90, Hut, Hut, Hut.

Some plays call for silent snap counts. This is more difficult and sometimes "false start" penalties are called on the offensive line.

Hard Counts are used to try to draw the defense offsides when short yardage is needed for a first down. The quarterback calls out the cadence, but the offensive line doesn't move, hoping the defense will jump forward ahead of time which results in a 5-yard penalty.

---

"At the line of scrimmage I always call out a play just before the ball is snapped. ... Now—if I want to change those instructions, I throw in a key number. The 'secret word' alerts them to the fact that I'm switching signals, and the play I am about to call is the one we will actually run."[ix]

*Charlie Conerly*
Former Quarterback
New York Giants

The offense has four plays called DOWNS to move the ball at least 10 yards by either passing or running the ball. If successful, they get a first down and are allowed another set of four plays to gain another 10 yards. This goes on until they score by crossing the goal line or they are stopped on four consecutive downs. If they are stopped on four consecutive downs, the offense may elect to punt the ball to the defense and then they swap roles. A typical play series might be something like this:

DOWNS

Each offensive play is a DOWN. The offense has four chances, or downs, to move the ball 10-yards in order to earn a first down. If they don't move the ball at least 10-yards, they go to the sidelines and their defense goes out on the field to play against the other team's offense.

FIRST PLAY: On first down the quarterback would hand off to the tailback who dives up the middle following his fullback that is blocking for him. He is tackled, only making 1 yard. Now it is second down and 9 yards to go for a first down—or "2nd and 9."

SECOND PLAY: The quarterback takes the snap and tosses the ball to the tailback who runs around the right side of the line and gains 3 yards. It is now third down and 6 yards to go for a first down—or "3rd and 6."

THIRD PLAY: The quarterback receives the snap and fades back to pass the ball, throws it to one of his receivers, but it is dropped, so it's an incomplete pass. Now it's FOURTH DOWN, and 6 yards to go—or "4th and 6."

FOURTH PLAY: The punt and the punt return teams enter the field. The center snaps the ball to the punter who is standing approximately twelve to fifteen yards behind him. He punts the ball and his team sprints downfield to tackle the punt returner (ball carrier). The punt return team blocks for their punt returner to help him gain as many yards as possible before he is tackled. When the ball carrier is down, the punt and punt return teams exit the field and the offense and defense teams enter.

## 4TH DOWN STRATEGIES

A team may elect to attempt a field goal worth 3 points if they have a kicker who is able to successfully kick the ball the distance required through the goal posts; or,

The offense elects to punt the ball because they are about to lose ball possession on the next down, therefore their best strategy is to place the ball as far away as possible from their end zone by punting. But if the offense tries to go for it and does not make the yardage required, the other team gains possession of the ball where the offensive player is tackled.

The defense's objective is to protect their end zone against the offense and gain possession of the ball. The plays the defense calls are based on the amount of yardage the offense has to gain for a first down and where the strength in the offense lies, in running or passing. If it is 3rd and 2 (third down and 2 yards to go) the offense may run the ball. Therefore, the defense's formation would require for more players on the line of scrimmage to stop the running play.

Teams swap end zones at the end of each quarter, thus changing their direction of play. At HALFTIME, players retire to their locker rooms to rest and re-group.

At the START OF THE SECOND HALF, the captains are called to midfield where the officials designate the team that kicked off will now be the receiving team. When the offensive team receives the kickoff, drives downfield, and is successful in crossing the goal line with the ball, a TOUCHDOWN is called and 6 points are earned.

They now have the option to either GO FOR 1 or 2 extra points. By placing the ball on the defender's extra point line, the place kicker must kick the ball between the goal post's uprights and over its crossbar. In order to "Go for 2," sometimes called a TWO POINT CONVERSION, the ball is placed on the defender's extra point line and in one play they must move the ball forward by either having a player carry the ball over or having the quarterback throw the ball to a teammate in the end zone to receive an additional 2 points.

The referee will call a TWO-MINUTE WARNING when there are only 2 minutes left in the game. The team with the most points at the end of the game wins.

FIVE WAYS TO SCORE

Touchdown — 6 points
    Extra Point — 1 point
    Two Point Conversion — 2 points
Field Goal — 3 points
Safety — 2 points

# THE

# X's and O's

## CHAPTER TEN

The X's and O's

The action on the football field may seem confusing, but every formation, play pattern, and strategy is planned and practiced. Coaches develop game plans and plays after assessing the opposing team's strengths and weaknesses. These strategies are diagramed in playbooks using an X to designate defensive players and an O to designate offensive players. The positions the players are set in are called "formations." After the huddle, the offensive and defensive teams get into their formations to execute the play call (or scheme) after the ball is snapped.

## OFFENSIVE FORMATIONS

The offense's objective is to move the ball down the field across their opponent's end zone, and score either by running or passing the ball or kicking the ball through the goal posts.

Seven players must be positioned on the line of scrimmage; five are linemen and two are eligible receivers. Once the offensive team is in set formation, they are not allowed to move for a full second before the snap, except for a single man in motion. The offense will either have a running or passing game, or a mixture of both, of which there are countless configurations created from basic offensive formations.

## BASIC OFFENSIVE FORMATIONS

I-FORMATION — the running backs are lined up directly behind the quarterback in the shape of an "I" so he can easily hand off the ball to one back and the other back block for him.

```
                                          ── LOS
   O        O O ◙ O O O
  WR        LT LG  C  RG RT TE      O
                   O               WR
                   QB

                   O FB
                   O TB      STRONG SIDE
```

T- FORMATION — the running backs are positioned behind the quarterback and off to either side, or split in the shape of a "T". This balanced formation is successful on running plays because the ball can be run or passed on both sides of the field.

```
                                        ── LOS
   O        O O ◙ O O O
  WR        LT LG  C  RG RT TE
                  O QB            O
                                 WR
             O      O
            FB      TB
```

SHOTGUN — the quarterback lines up 5-7 yards behind the center. This gives him a better view of the defense and a few seconds more to search the field for an open receiver and immediately throw the ball without having to drop back.

```
                                        ── LOS
   O        O  O ◙ O O O
  WR        LT LG C RG RT TE
                         O       O
                 O FB   HB      WR
             O
             QB
```

## OFFENSIVE HOLE NUMBERS AND PLAY CALLS

The spaces or HOLES in-between the players on the offensive line are numbered: odd numbers on the center's left and even on the center's right.

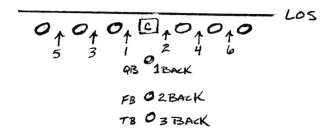

An offensive play call might be two numbers and a word description. For example, if the quarterback called "22 DIVE," the quarterback's handing the ball off to the #2 back to run the ball through the #2 hole. The linemen on either side of the #2 hole will know the back is running in-between them, therefore they must block their defensive players in order to create the hole for the ball carrier.

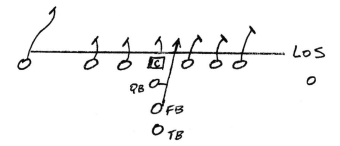

If the quarterback is said to be "in the pocket," it means the area where the quarterback stands is protected by his offensive line, therefore he is in a "pocket of protection."

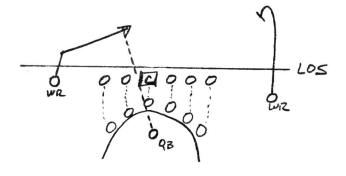

## OFFENSIVE PASS PATTERNS

Every team has its own pass routes or passing patterns that receivers run during a play to give the quarterback the best chance to complete a pass. Routes vary with the quarterback and receiver's arm strength and skill. These passing routes are assigned numbers and names for the receivers to memorize and be able to put into action on the playing field. Receivers run different routes in order to confuse the defense and allow the quarterback to find the best open receiver to successfully complete the pass.

### BASIC OFFENSIVE PASS PATTERNS

- POST — a receiver runs directly downfield toward the goal posts for a long pass.
- CURL — a receiver runs about 5 to 10 yards beyond the line of scrimmage, steps and turns back toward the quarterback to catch the ball.
- SLANT — a receiver is aligned from the offensive line's tight end or tackle. The receiver runs straight for about 5 yards and then angles across the field.

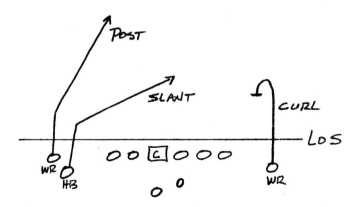

# BASIC OFFENSIVE PASS PATTERNS (cont.)

- HOOK — the receiver runs downfield about 10 yards and suddenly turns to receive the ball that the quarterback has already released.

- FLY — the receiver quickly runs downfield and the quarterback throws him a deep pass.

- DOWN and OUT — the receiver runs downfield about 5 to 10 yards and cuts out toward the sideline to catch the ball.

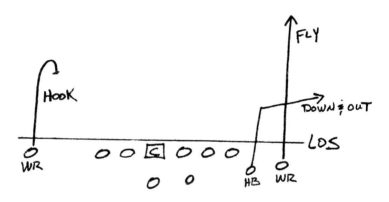

## OFFENSIVE RUNNING PLAYS

A wide variety of running plays exist where the quarterback, fullback, or tailback (halfback) run with the ball. The linemen open "holes" for the ball carrier to run through.

## BASIC OFFENSIVE RUNNING PLAYS

- DIVE — a quick play where the quarterback hands off to the fullback to run up the middle in the hole between the center and the guard.

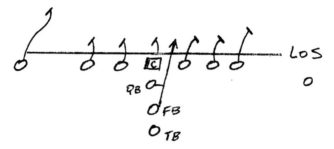

- REVERSE — the quarterback hands off the ball to the tailback who unexpectedly hands off the ball to the wide receiver running in the opposite direction.

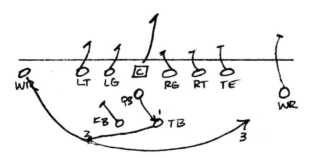

- OFF TACKLE — the quarterback hands off to the tail back to run through a hole between the offensive tackle and the end. The tailback runs wide around the strong side (with the tight end) covered by the tackle and end.

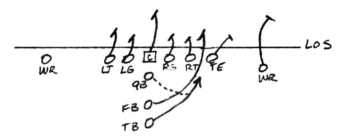

- SWEEP — the quarterback tosses the ball to the tail back to run parallel to the line of scrimmage.

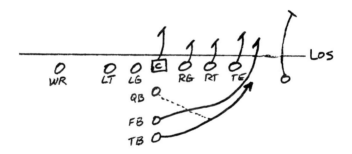

- OPTION — the quarterback has the option to either keep and run the ball or pass it laterally to the tailback.

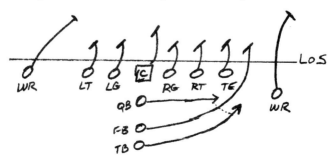

## DEFENSIVE FORMATIONS

The defense's objective is to stop the offense from advancing and to gain possession of the ball. The opposing team's offensive strength and the yardage to be gained factor into the formations and strategies the coaches will put into play.

There is no requirement for a specific number of defensive players to be positioned on the line of scrimmage as required on the offense. The number of linemen and linebackers on the line of scrimmage and the number of linebackers behind them determine the name of the plays, called "fronts." A 4-3 front, or 4-3 defense, is interpreted as four linemen and three linebackers, with four defensive backs.

## BASIC DEFENSIVE FORMATIONS

4-3 DEFENSE — works against a passing offense.

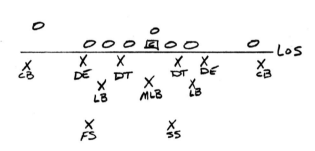

NICKEL DEFENSE — five defensive backs to protect against a passing offense.

5-2 DEFENSE — works against a running offense.

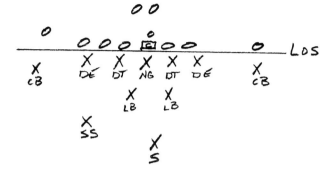

5-3 DEFENSE — works against both a passing and running offense.

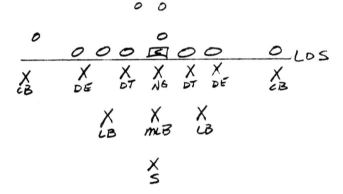

GOAL LINE DEFENSE — works against a passing or running offense.

# DEFENSIVE STRATEGIES

● ZONE DEFENSE — the linebackers and defensive backs wait for the offense to move into specific areas they are assigned to defend.

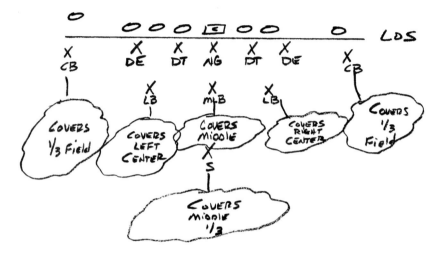

● MAN-to-MAN — each defensive back is assigned to cover a specific offensive receiver.

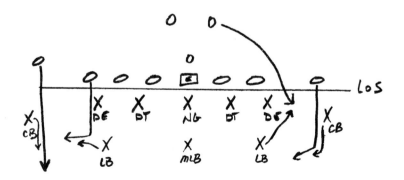

STUNT — the defensive linemen and linebackers "shoot the gap" to disrupt the play and tackle the ball carrier.

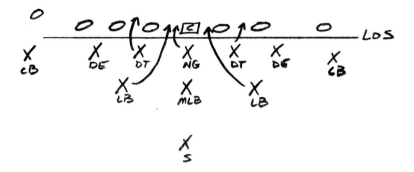

BLITZ — the defensive linemen and defensive backs "rush the quarterback" at one time to "sack the quarterback" or force him to make a bad throw.

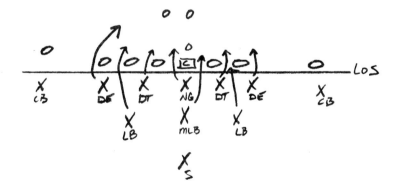

## SPECIAL TEAM X's and O's

ONSIDE KICK — If it is late in the game, the losing team may choose an onside kick if they need to quickly regain possession of the ball. On kickoff, the ball is kicked short to try to allow the kicking team to recover the ball before the receiving team, but it must be kicked at least 10 yards.

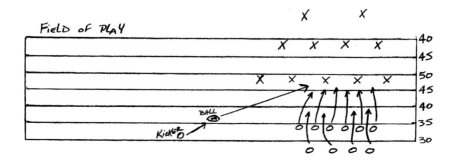

## SPECIAL TEAM X's and O's

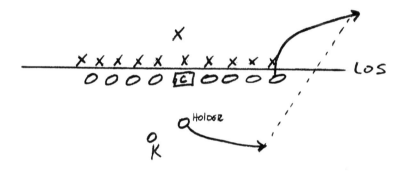 FAKE FIELD GOAL and FAKE PUNT — A team
that is behind in the score may choose to use this
strategy to regain possession of the ball. On fourth
down, the offense lines up as if going for a field
goal, but tries for a first down instead. The holder or
the punter takes the snap and either runs with it or
passes it to a receiver.

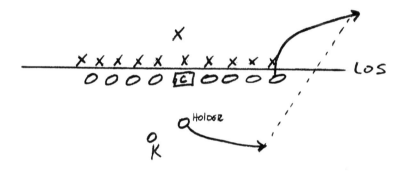

Touchdown
Field Goal, Extra Point

SAFETY

START CLOCK

TOUCHBACK

INComplete PASS
No GooD

Delay of GAME

HoldinG

ILLEGAL USE OF HANDS

ILLEGAL RECEIVER
DOWNFiELd

LOSS of DOWN

FACE MASK

CliPPiNG

TIME OUT

FIRST DOWN

PERSONAL FOUL

FALSE START

OFF SIDES

ILLEGAL MOTION

INTENTIONAL GROUNDING

PASS INTERFENCE

TRIPPING

ILLEGAL BLOCK

ROUGHING THE KICKER

UNSPORTSMANlIKE CONDUCT

# Gridiron Glossary

# The Gridiron Glossary

**AUDIBLE** — a play-change shouted by the quarterback at the line of scrimmage.

**BALL CARRIER** — a player holding, and in control of, the ball.

**BACK** — a member of the offensive or defensive backfield.

**BACKFIELD** — 1) the set of players on offense or defense that set up behind their linemen; 2) the area behind both the offensive and defensive lines.

**BALANCED LINE** — an equal number of offensive linemen are on either side of the center at the line of scrimmage.

**BLIND-SIDED** — a player is hit from the direction opposite his view, his "blind side."

**BLITZ** — a defensive strategy when one or more of the linebackers and defensive backs charge through the offensive line attempting to tackle the quarterback before he passes or hands off the ball.

**BLOCKING** — when offensive players use their bodies to stop defensive players without holding onto the opposing player, trying to bring the ball carrier to the ground (a tackle).

BOMB — a ball passed long and hard to a receiver downfield.

BOOTLEG — the quarterback fakes a handoff to a running back and then runs the ball around one end of the line of scrimmage.

BOX — an imaginary area near the line of scrimmage where most defensive linemen and linebackers stand prior to the beginning of a play.

BREAKING THE PLANE — if the ball carrier crosses an imaginary line above the opponent's goal line (the plane), a score is awarded to the offense.

CATCH — to obtain possession of a live ball in the air.

CENTER — the middle offensive lineman who begins each play by exchanging the ball between his legs (the "snap" or "hike") to the quarterback, kick holder, or punter; he may also be known as the "snapper."

CHAIN CREW — three official assistants that measure an offense's progress toward getting four new efforts (turns) to advance the ball (called "downs"); they use a 10-yard chain and a marker counting the number of downs.

CLIPPING — hitting an opponent's backside; this causes a 15-yard penalty.

CHOP BLOCK — blocking an opponent's backside below the opponent's waist; this causes a 15-yard penalty.

CORNERBACK — a player in the defense's secondary (rear players on defense) that guard the right or left third of the field from passes.

COUNT — the quarterback's verbal commands to the center to snap (hike) him the ball. Sometimes, only physical gestures are used.

COUNTER — an offensive back runs one direction, then hands the ball to a back running the opposite way.

CURL ROUTE — a receiver runs several yards past the line of scrimmage, stops and turns (curls) toward the quarterback, who passes him the ball.

CUTBACK — a back carries the ball one direction in the backfield, then "cuts back" the other way across the line of scrimmage.

DEAD BALL — the play is over.

DEEP — a long pass.

DEFENSE — the 11-player squad trying to stop the offense and to gain possession of the ball.

DEFENSIVE BACKS — three to four players composed of the free safety, strong safety, and cornerbacks, called the "defensive backfield," whose objective is: 1) to stop receivers from catching a pass and; 2) to make tackles.

DEFENSIVE LINEMEN — composed of the nose tackle (or nose guard), defensive tackles, and defensive ends positioned across the line of scrimmage from the offensive linemen. Defensive linemen try to tackle the offensive ball carrier.

DEFENSIVE TACKLE — a defensive lineman that is usually positioned opposite each offensive guard or tackle.

DEFENSIVE END — a defensive lineman positioned opposite the offensive tackle or end.

DELAY OF GAME — the offense fails to begin a play within a set time period; a 5-yard penalty and the down must be repeated.

DIME BACK — a sixth defensive back positioned to help stop the offense's passing game.

DIME DEFENSE — a defensive backfield formation that adds a sixth defensive back (dime back) to help stop passing plays.

DIVE — a quick offensive running play up the middle in the gap between the center and the guard or the guard and the tackle.

DOUBLE-TEAM — when two offensive linemen block the same defender or when two defensive players challenge the same offensive player.

DOWN — one in a series of four offensive plays to advance the football 10 yards and keep possession of the ball. If successful, a team gets four more downs; if not, the other team gets the ball and four downs.

DOWNING THE BALL — a player kneels with the ball after catching a kick or punt in his own end zone; the player is saying he will not run the ball forward and wants to start his offense's efforts on the 20-yard line.

DRAW — the quarterback backs up from the center (called "fading back") as if to throw to a receiver, but then hands the ball to a running back, or runs the ball himself.

DRIVE — a series of plays in which the offense moves the ball down the field toward a score.

DUMMY — big pads that simulate opposing players, and are used to practice tackling and blocking.

END LINE — the horizontal boundary line that marks the rear end of the end zone.

END ZONE — the legal area between the goal line, end line and sidelines where a player can score a touchdown; it measures 10 yards deep.

ENDS — the player lined outside the offensive tackle that blocks or receives passes; tight ends, wide receivers, wide outs or split ends all are "ends."

EXTRA POINT(S) — a team scoring a 6-point touchdown normally chooses to place kick for 1 more point, called an extra point; the kicker boots the ball (held on end by the holder) through the goal posts; two extra points can be scored by running or passing the ball into the end zone from the 3-yard line, called a 2-point conversion, which is riskier.

EXTRA POINT TEAM — the 11-player team trying to score extra points after a 6-point touchdown; the football is kicked through the goal posts to earn 1 extra point or a team may choose to try to run or pass the ball into the end zone from the 3-yard line to score a 2-point conversion.

FACEMASK — when a player intentionally grabs an opponent's facemask attached to the helmet, it is a 15-yard penalty and automatic first down; when a player unintentionally grabs an opponent's facemask, it is a 5-yard penalty and the down is repeated.

FADE BACK — a quarterback backs up after receiving the ball from the center, looking to throw the ball.

FAIR CATCH — a player may receive a punt or kick without being tackled by quickly waving his hand above his head before catching the ball; he is promising not to run with the ball once it is caught; an unsuccessful fair catch, however, results in a live ball.

FALSE START — an offensive player illegally moves before the ball is snapped from the center to quarterback, resulting in a 5-yard penalty.

FIELD GOAL — a successful kick of the ball through the U-shaped goal posts; this is worth 3 points.

FIELD GOAL TEAM — a group of 11 players whose specialty is blocking for the kicker while he is attempting to kick the field goal.

FIELD POSITION — the location of the ball between offensive plays on the 100-yard field.

FIRST DOWN — the first in a series of four offensive attempts—1st, 2nd, 3rd, 4th downs—to move the ball toward the opponent's end zone; the offense is allowed four attempts to gain a total of 10 yards.

FLAG — a bright yellow cloth that officials keep in their back hip pocket to pull out and throw on the ground, signaling there has been a penalty.

FLANKER — an extra running back positioned just behind the end of the offense's tight end; this also called a wingback.

FLOATER — a term used to describe a ball that hangs in the air due to lack of velocity.

FLY ROUTE — a receiver runs straight and fast down the field to receive a deep pass.

FOOTBALL — a prolate spheroid that is made of four panels of grained leather sewn with a row of white laces.

FORCE OUT — when a receiver jumps up to catch a ball in the air and is forced out of bounds before both feet can land in bounds; it is ruled a complete pass.

FORMATION — an arrangement of players on the football field at the start of the play.

FORWARD PASS — a ball thrown in the direction of the opponent's goal line.

FORWARD PROGRESS — the full distance a ball carrier moved the ball down the field.

FOUL — a rule infraction punishable by a penalty.

FREE KICK — if a team gives up a safety (their player is tackled in their own end zone) they must punt the ball from their own 20-yard-line to their opposition.

FULLBACK — a running back that is positioned behind the quarter-back to block, catch a pass, or run the ball.

FUMBLE — a ball carrier drops the ball before the play ends; who-ever recovers the live ball—either on offense or defense—is awarded offensive possession.

GAP — the space between the offensive linemen through which the ball is designed to be carried; the defense tries to enter the gaps to pre-vent forward motion of the offense.

GAME PLAN — the strategy of plays and formations designed by the coaches to defeat their opponents.

GOAL LINE — the line at either end of the 100-yard playing field that a player must cross with the ball to score, either by running or catching the ball.

GOALPOST — one of two upright posts joined by a crossbar into a large U and positioned at the back of each end zone; teams kick the ball between these "uprights" to score a 3-point field goal or 1 extra point.

"GOING FOR IT" — when the offense decides on 4th down to run or pass the ball to try to make a new first down, instead of turning the ball over to the other team's offense by a punt.

GRIDIRON — the football field historically has had many lines marking it, resembling a pattern or grid, thus the term "gridiron."

GUARD — the offensive linemen on either side of the center (the middle offensive lineman); their objective is to block defensive linemen, linebackers and ends.

HAIL MARY — a quarterback's deep pass toward the end zone with hopes that one of his receivers will catch the ball.

HALFBACK — the primary offensive running back, who also catches balls and blocks defensive players; also known as the tailback.

HALFTIME — the rest period for teams between the second and third quarters.

HAND-OFF —a quarterback gives, or hands, the ball to another back to advance it.

HANG TIME — the amount of time a ball that is punted remains in flight; greater hang time reduces an opposition's chance to catch and return it.

HARD COUNT — a verbal cadence the quarterback calls out to his teammates at the line of scrimmage, used to attempt to draw the defense offsides.

HASH MARKS — broken lines in one-yard increments down the middle of the playing field that define the area where all plays must start; when a play ends near a sideline or out of bounds the ball is centered on the nearest hash mark.

HIKE — the backward movement of the ball from the center's hands to the hands of the quarterback behind him; also called a "snap."

HOLE — the space between defensive linemen that offensive linemen try to create for their backs to run with the ball.

HOLDER — a player assigned to hold the ball for the kicker to kick.

HOLDING — a player illegally grabs an opposing player; a 10-yard offensive penalty or 5-yard defensive penalty.

HOME FIELD ADVANTAGE — the benefit to a team from playing on its home field, due to field familiarity, more fan support and no travel time.

HUDDLE — before each play, players briefly gather to receive the play instructions from the quarterback on the offense, and the middle linebacker on the defense.

"I" FORMATION —when two offensive backs line up behind the quarterback to form the shape of an "I," normally with the intent of running the ball.

IN BOUNDS — the playing area inside the end lines and sidelines on a field.

IN THE FLATS — the open areas near sidelines and the line of scrimmage where the ball is sometimes thrown to receivers.

IN THE GRASP — a defensive player retains a quarterback in his own backfield long enough for officials to rule a tackle, stopping the play and preventing injury to the quarterback.

IN THE SEAM — an open area between defensive backs that receivers try to find to become open for a pass.

INCOMPLETE PASS — a thrown ball that is not caught.

INELIGIBLE RECEIVER — an offensive lineman on a passing play (wearing a jersey numbered 50-79) who crosses the line of scrimmage and advances downfield before the ball is thrown; the penalty is 5 yards.

ILLEGAL BLOCK — a player impedes an opponent below the waist during an interception, fumble recovery, or kicking play; a 15 yard penalty and automatic first down.

ILLEGAL PROCEDURE — an offense's wrongful shift of players or formation of players; a 5-yard penalty.

ILLEGAL USE OF HANDS—if an offensive player inappropriately pushes or pulls the ball carrier forward, or hits his opponent in the head or neck to prevent a tackle, it is a 10-yard penalty and the down is repeated; or, if a defensive player inappropriately grabs or pulls an offensive player, it is a 5-yard penalty and an automatic first down for the offense.

INSTANT REPLAY RULING — an approved review of an official's ruling regarding a play that was challenged by a coach.

INTENTIONAL GROUNDING — the quarterback, knowing there are no receivers to catch the ball, intentionally throws an incomplete pass to avoid being tackled; this means a 5-yard penalty is given and the down is repeated.

INTERCEPTION — a defensive player catches a pass intended for an offensive player; the intercepting team gets ball possession.

INTERFERENCE — an offensive receiver or defensive player is hit, tackled, or grabbed before receiving a pass; a first down for the offense at the site of the foul; or, a 10-yard penalty for the defense.

KEYING ON — to closely watch a particular player to decide in which direction he will move.

KICKER — the most important special team players; the place kicker is responsible for kickoffs, extra points and field goals.

KICKOFF — a player kicks the ball off of a tee to begin the game, to begin the second half, and after each score.

KICKOFF TEAM — a special team of 11 players that try to tackle the player who catches the kicked ball.

KICK RETURN TEAM — a special team of 11 players, 10 of which try to protect their kicker by blocking defenders.

KICKING GAME — offensive strategies that involve placekicking and punting against the opposing receiving team.

LATERAL — a sideways or backward toss from one player to another player, who then advances the ball.

LINEBACKER — a defensive player that stands behind the defensive linemen and runs to tackle the back or receiver carrying the ball.

LINE OF SCRIMMAGE (LOS) — two imaginary lines for each team that are separated by the length of the ball, called the neutral zone; teams can't cross the LOS prior to the snap.

LIVE BALL — a ball during an active play that momentarily is not held by any player.

LOOSE BALL — a ball that has been fumbled (dropped), prior to either team grabbing hold of it.

MAN IN MOTION — an offensive back or receiver legally moving parallel or away from the line of scrimmage prior to a play starting.

MAN-TO-MAN — a defender is assigned to one specific offensive player.

MIDFIELD — the football field's 50-yard line is the exact middle point between the two end zones.

NEUTRAL ZONE — the area between the offensive and defensive lines positioned at the line of scrimmage, as wide as the length of the football, from tip to tip. The offensive center is the only player allowed to enter the neutral zone before the play begins.

NICKEL BACK — a fifth defensive back who stops ball carriers running around the end of the line, and receivers trying to catch short passes; this is also known as a plugger.

NICKEL DEFENSE — a defensive backfield with a fifth back (nickel back) to stop the offense's passing game.

NOSE GUARD (NOSE TACKLE) — a defensive lineman who positions himself across the football from the offensive center.

OFFENSE — a squad of 11 players opposite the defense trying to pass or run the ball down the field into their opponent's end zone.

OFFENSIVE BACKS — members of the offensive backfield composed of the quarterback and running backs: fullback, halfback or tailback, wingback or flanker.

OFFICIALS — a crew of four to seven men who enforce the rules of the football game; the referee, umpire, head linesman, line judge, side judge, back judge and field judge all have distinct responsibilities and field positions.

OFF SIDES — an offensive player moves past the resting ball at the line of scrimmage before a play starts, or a defensive player moves past the resting ball and does not return to a set position before the play starts; this causes a 5-yard penalty on offense or defense.

OFF-TACKLE — the running back runs off the outside shoulder of the offensive tackle.

ONSIDE KICK — a short kickoff that must travel at least 10 yards, after which the kicking team tries to catch or cover the ball to regain possession; this is often used at the end of close games.

OPTION — a quarterback is running parallel to the line of scrimmage and chooses either to run up the field or to toss (pitch) the ball back to another back.

OSKY — an interception by a defensive player.

OUT OF BOUNDS — when a ball is carried or thrown out of the field of play, it is out of bounds.

OVERTIME — an extension of playing time to determine the winner in a tied game.

PASS — a ball thrown forward to a receiver; a pass caught by a receiver is "complete"; a pass not caught by a receiver is "incomplete."

PASS DEFENDER — a defensive player who shadows an offensive receiver to keep him from catching the ball.

PASS INTERFERENCE — a receiver is hit, tackled or grabbed by a defender before the ball reaches the receiver.

PASS PATTERN — one of many planned routes receivers run down the field to get away from defenders so their quarterback can throw the ball to them.

PASS PROTECTION — when offensive players block defenders from interfering with the quarterback's passing play.

PASS RUSH — when defensive players try to tackle or obstruct the quarterback attempting to pass the ball downfield.

PASSING GAME — the offensive strategies to transfer the ball from one player to another by throwing and receiving it.

PENALTIES — the punishment for a rules violation.

PERSONAL FOUL — harmful force used by one player against another; this means a 15-yard penalty is given and the down is repeated.

PICK OFF — a pass caught by a defender instead of the intended offensive receiver; also called an interception.

PITCHOUT — the quarterback tosses the ball behind him to the running back.

PLACEKICK — a holder stands the football on end and the kicker boots it through the goal posts.

PLAY — the game strategies that start with a kick or a snap and finish with a dead ball.

PLAY ACTION PASS — the quarterback fakes giving the ball to someone, and then passes the ball to someone else.

PLAY CLOCK — the clock at each end zone showing everyone the time (25 to 0 seconds) between two downs before a new offensive play must begin.

PREVENT DEFENSE — a defensive strategy using only three or four linemen, freeing up seven or eight players in the defensive backfield to prevent long passes.

POCKET — the area where a quarterback stands, protected by his offensive line, to throw a pass; he is in a "pocket of protection" or "in the pocket."

POINT AFTER TOUCHDOWN — (P.A.T.), a placekick that equals one point after a 6-point touchdown; it is also called an extra point.

POOCH KICK —a ball is dropped on the foot and punted in a short, high fashion to make it stop on the field before entering the opposing team's end zone; if the ball enters the end zone, the opposing team gets to start offense on their 20-yard line.

POSSESSION — a term referring to being in control of the ball.

PUNT — a ball is dropped on a player's (punter's) foot and booted as far down the field as possible.

PUNT TEAM — a special team with the punter and ten other players; they boot the ball as far down the field as possible to a receiver, then try to tackle the receiver; the punt team is used mostly on an offense's fourth down.

PUNT RETURN TEAM — a special team with a receiver and ten other players; the receiver catches a punted ball while the other ten block for him to run up the field; the punt return team is used regularly on fourth down.

PUNTER — the offensive player who drops the ball onto his foot, kicking it far down field.

PYLON — an orange marker at each corner of both end zones.

QUARTER — the four time periods—1st, 2nd, 3rd, 4th quarter—of a football game.

QUARTERBACK (QB) — the offensive leader who runs or throws the ball to teammates; he communicates each play to his offense, and starts each play by taking the ball (a snap) from his center.

QUARTERBACK SNEAK — the quarterback takes the ball from his center (a snap) and runs straight ahead; used mostly when a few yards are needed for a first down.

READING THE DEFENSE — a skill developed by the quarterback to recognize the defense's positioning; after "reading," he may decide to alter his offensive play by calling an audible to his teammates prior to the snap.

RECEIVER — an offensive player whose primary role is to catch forward passes; includes wide receivers, tight ends, wingbacks, or "flankers."

RECOVER — to reclaim possession of a live ball on the ground or in the air.

RED FLAG — in professional football only, a head coach may toss a red flag to challenge an official's ruling; then, a review is made using TV instant replay; the replay may reverse the official's call and benefit the head coach or it may uphold the official's call and the head coach's team loses a time out.

RED ZONE — an unmarked area between the end zone and 20-yard line in which teams emphasize their ability to score and to stop others from scoring.

RETURN — a player catches a punt or kickoff and tries to advance the ball toward his opponent's goal line.

REVERSE — a back runs with the ball to one side of the field, coaxing the defense to follow, but then hands the ball to another teammate running in the opposite direction.

ROLL OUT — a quarterback runs right or left of the line of scrimmage looking to throw to a receiver downfield.

ROOKIE — a player's first year.

ROSTER — the list of the members on the team.

ROUGHING THE KICKER/PUNTER — a defensive player hits the kicker/punter as he is kicking the ball and a 15-yard penalty is given as well as an automatic first down.

RUNNING BACK — an offensive player whose primary responsibility is to carry the ball and gain as much yardage as possible; this includes a fullback, tailback (halfback), wingback (flanker).

RUSH — an offensive runner advances the ball forward; or, a defensive player crosses the line of scrimmage in aggressive pursuit of the quarterback.

SACK — a quarterback is brought to the ground in his backfield by a defensive player; if two players sack a quarterback, each is credited with 1/2 a sack.

SAFETY — 1) a defensive back responsible for stopping receivers running in the middle third of the backfield or those running long pass routes; 2) a play in which a ball carrier is brought to the ground in his own end zone, earning the defense 2 points and forcing the offense to kick the ball to the defense from the offense's 20-yard line.

SCHEME — the offensive and defensive formations and strategies for playing football.

SCOUT REPORT — a description of the opposing team's strengths and weaknesses.

SCRAMBLE — a quarterback runs outside of the pocket to avoid being tackled.

SCREEN — a quarterback backs up from center with the ball and looks to throw the ball downfield, coaxing defensive players his way; then he throws a short pass to his right or left over the fooled defensive linemen.

SCRIMMAGE — a practice game.

SECONDARY — the entire set of defensive players—the free safety, strong safety, and cornerbacks—covering offensive receivers.

SET POSITION — offensive linemen must stay still in a ready position before the ball is put into play (snapped).

SHIFT — when an offensive back, defensive back, or a defensive lineman changes places on the field before the ball is put into play (snapped).

SHOTGUN — an offensive formation where the quarterback lines up four to seven feet behind the center and takes a long snap, allowing him more time to throw the ball.

SHOOTING THE GAP — a defensive player tries to run through a space between the offensive linemen.

SIDELINE — the boundary line that runs lengthwise down both sides of the playing field.

SIGNALS — the instructions called by the quarterback to the offensive players at the line of scrimmage.

SNAP — the center either hands or hikes the ball between his legs to the quarterback to start a play.

SNAPPER — an offensive player specializing in hiking the ball between his legs to the kicker, kick holder or quarterback.

SNAP COUNT — a secret code the quarterback calls to his teammates to start a play; an example is "Red 90, Hut, Hut, Hut."

SPECIAL TEAMS — the squad of 11 players specializing in executing kicking plays.

SPIRAL — a football's tight spin in flight.

SPLIT END — a receiver lined up outside the offensive tackles, in most cases to catch passes; this is also known as a wide receiver or a wide out.

SQUIB KICK — a ball intentionally kicked to flutter and roll erratically in hopes of causing the receiving team to fumble it.

STANCE — a player's ready position that helps him move with ease and quickness.

STOPPAGE — a stop of the game clock because: 1) a play is over, 2) a timeout has been called, or 3) another official reason.

STRAIGHT- OR STIFF-ARM — a ball carrier legally pushes off a would-be tackler with his arm.

STRIPPING THE BALL — a player forces the ball out of ball carrier's grasp.

STRONG SIDE — the side of the offensive formation where the tight end is positioned.

STUNTS — when linebackers and/or defensive ends rush quickly into the offensive backfield to disrupt an offensive play.

SUBSTITUTION — one player replacing another between two plays; if a team has more than 11 players on the field when the play starts, it is an illegal substitution.

SWEEP — a ball carrier runs around his offensive line, instead of through it, to advance the ball.

TACKLES — the offensive linemen positioned outside the guards, and on either side of the nose guard on defense.

TACKLE — when a defensive player hits or pulls a ball carrier to the ground to stop a play.

TAILGATE — a gathering of football fans outside a stadium to eat, drink, socialize and discuss the game.

THROWING THE BALL AWAY — an intentional incomplete pass by the quarterback to avoid being tackled.

TIGHT END — an offensive player positioned beside the tackle that specializes in receiving passes and blocking with the offensive line; the side that the tight end lines up on is called the strong side.

TIME-OUT — a stop of the game clock by a team to recoup or strategize; each team is allowed three time-outs per half.

TOUCHBACK — a situation in which a player gets possession of the ball in his own end zone through a punt, kickoff, or interception; he downs the ball in his own end zone by kneeling on the ground on one knee; his team is awarded possession of the ball, and their offense starts on its own 20-yard line with a first down.

TOUCHDOWN — the main objective of each team and worth 6 points; achieved by crossing the defender's goal line with possession of the ball by either running the ball, catching a pass or falling on a live ball.

TRIPPING — a player is intentionally tripped by the opposition to gain an advantage, resulting in a 10-yard penalty and a loss of a down.

TURNOVER — possession of the ball changes between teams due to a fumble, an interception, or an onside kick.

TWO-MINUTE WARNING — a signal given by the officials to let the teams know that two minutes remain in a half.

TWO-POINT CONVERSION — an offense scores 2 extra points after a touchdown by running or throwing the ball across the goal line from the 3-yard line; because it is riskier, this is chosen less than kicking for 1 extra-point.

UNBALANCED LINE — a different number of offensive players line up on either the right or left side of the center.

UNSPORTSMANLIKE CONDUCT — a player verbally or physically demeans or threatens an opponent, official or fan; a 15-yard penalty and automatic first down are awarded.

THE UPRIGHTS — the two U-shaped posts of the goal at the back of either end zone through which a ball must be kicked to score either 3 points (a field goal) or 1 point (an extra point).

WEAK SIDE — the offensive side of the ball that is opposite where the tight end is positioned.

WEST COAST OFFENSE — a style of offensive play utilizing many short passing strategies and creative running plays.

WIDE RECEIVER — a receiver positioned far away from the offensive line, near the sidelines; this includes a wide out or split end.

WING BACK — an extra running back positioned behind the tight end's outside shoulder whose objective is to receive passes; this is also known as a "flanker."

X'S AND O'S — a series of offensive plays and defensive formations that coaches develop to form their team's game plans.

YAC — the number of yards a receiver runs with the ball after catching it; "yards after catch."

YARD LINES — the lines on the field divided in 5-yard increments.

YARDAGE — the number of yards gained or lost during a play.

ZONE DEFENSE — all defensive backs are assigned specific areas of the field in which to protect against the offense.

# Football Field Diagram

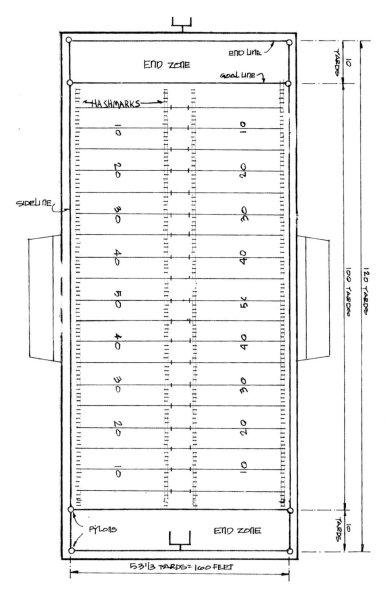

END LINE
END ZONE
GOAL LINE
10 YARDS
HASHMARKS
10
20
30
40
50
40
30
20
10
SIDELINE
10
20
30
40
50
40
30
20
10
100 YARDS
120 YARDS
END ZONE
10 YARDS
PYLONS
53 1/3 YARDS = 160 FEET

# Endnotes

[i] http://www.fritzpollard.com, accessed 9/20/05.

[ii] http://waltercamp.org/history5.htm, accessed 9/20/05.

[iii] *The Life Application Bible*, New International Version © 1988, 1990, 1991 by Tyndale House Publishers, Inc. and Zondervan Publishing House.

[iv] www.google.com/u/USAFootball?1=quotes,accessed, 10/17/05.

[v] http://coachlikeapro.tripod.com/basketball/id14.html, accessed 10/02/06.

[vi] http://www.woopidoo.com/business_quotes/goal-quotes.htm, accessed 10/02/06.

[vii] http://www.cybernationvictory/quotations/subjects/quotes competition.html, accessed 2/17/05.

[viii] source unknown.

[ix] Perian Conerly, *Backseat Quarterback*, (Garden City, NY: Doubleday & Company, Inc., 1963) 112.